THE LOST LAMB
AND THE GOOD
THE SHEPHERD

written by **DANDI DALEY MACKALL**

illustrated by **LISA MANUZAK**

TYNDALE
K!DS

TYNDALE HOUSE PUBLISHERS, INC.
CAROL STREAM, IL

flipside
STORIES

To Cassie Hendren,
with love forever!

Visit Tyndale's website for kids at www.tyndale.com/kids.

TYNDALE is a registered trademark of Tyndale House Publishers, Inc. The Tyndale Kids logo is a trademark of Tyndale House Publishers, Inc.

The Lost Lamb and the Good Shepherd

Copyright © 2016 by Dandi A. Mackall. All rights reserved.

Illustrations copyright © Lisa Manuzak. All rights reserved.

Designed by Jacqueline L. Nuñez

Edited by Stephanie Rische

Scripture quotations are taken from the *Holy Bible*, New Living Translation, copyright © 1996, 2004, 2015 by Tyndale House Foundation. Used by permission of Tyndale House Publishers, Inc., Carol Stream, Illinois 60188. All rights reserved.

For manufacturing information regarding this product, please call 1-800-323-9400.

ISBN 978-1-4964-1121-1

Printed in China

22	21	20	19	18	17	16
7	6	5	4	3	2	1

THE LOST LAMB'S SIDE OF THE STORY

I'm one in a hundred of white,
    woolly sheep
Who stay by the Shepherd,
    awake or asleep.

3

But one day I dreamed of new fields, lush and green.
I'd surely be happy in that lovely scene.

I took off a-trotting and plotting escape,
My plan for green pastures was now taking shape.

5

I followed a path winding left, curving right.
Then thunderclouds BOOMED, and a storm hit the
   night.

I ran for some bushes, but thorns scraped my back.
My stomach was grumbling. The sky had turned black.

I heard in the distance the screech of an owl,
The growl of a bear, and a wily wolf's howl.

Oh, why did I leave? Now I'm lost and alone.
No Shepherd to guide me—no fault but my own.

I shuffled through brambles. I rambled and
   stumbled.
My hooves slipped and slid. Down the cliff side I
   tumbled!

I clung to a branch. I was weak in the knees. And that's when I cried, "Help me! Somebody, please!"

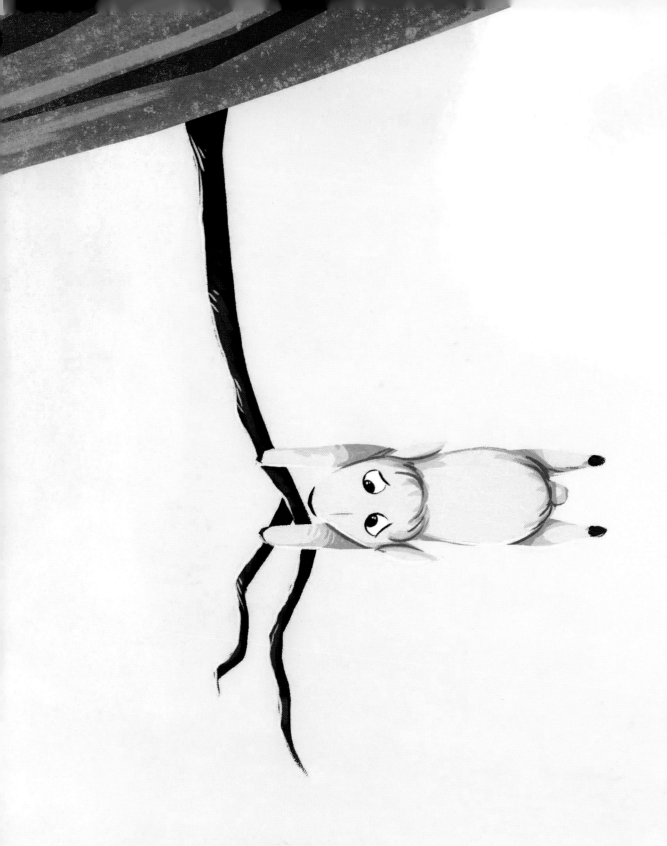

But why would the Good Shepherd answer my plea?
With ninety-nine sheep, who would care about me?

"Don't worry! I'm coming! I know that you're lost.
But trust Me to find you, whatever the cost."

19

And then the Good Shepherd reached out His
  strong arm.

He brought me to safety and kept me from harm.

The Good Shepherd saved me! He carried me back.
Now I am His lamb, safe and sound, back on track.

23

THE GOOD SHEPHERD'S SIDE OF THE STORY

I'm the Good Shepherd of one hundred sheep.
I find them green pastures, keep watch while they
   sleep.

I know them by name, and I call them My own.
I hear every *baa*, every bleat, every moan.

Then one day I counted,
and something was wrong!
"O littlest lamb, you're not
where you belong."

I called, but no answer. I
grew more concerned.
I promised that I would
leave no stone unturned.

I left the whole flock and went searching for one
Who'd wandered astray, like a prodigal son.

9

Some shepherds might say, "You've still got
 ninety-nine."
But how could I leave one? The lost lamb was Mine.

I ran down the hill and then over the top.
The thunder and lightning could not make Me stop.

My poor little lamb! How I wish he'd obeyed.
My lost little lamb, all alone and afraid.

And that's when I heard the most desperate cries.
"I'm coming!" I said—and I never tell lies.

15

My lamb was in danger! He hung by a thread.
I pulled him to safety and kissed his sweet head.

"There, there, little lamb. You were frightened, I know.
No matter what happens, I won't let you go."

I carried My lamb, safe and sound, to our flock.
For I'm the Good Shepherd, your Friend and your
Rock.

Rejoice with me because I have found my lost sheep.

LUKE 15:6

WAIT!
YOU THOUGHT YOU WERE FINISHED, DIDN'T YOU?

IT'S TIME TO TAKE ANOTHER LOOK!
CLOSE THEN FLIP
THIS STORYBOOK!